Contemplating Jesus

Contemplating Jesus

Robert Faricy, S.J.
and
Robert J. Wicks

Paulist Press
New York/Mahwah

Copyright © 1986 by
Robert Faricy and Robert J. Wicks

All rights reserved. No part of this book may be reproduced or transmitted in any form or by any means, electronic or mechanical, including photocopying, recording or by any information storage and retrieval system without permission in writing from the Publisher.

Library of Congress
Catalog Card Number: 85-62864

ISBN: 0-8091-2757-1

Published by Paulist Press
997 Macarthur Boulevard
Mahwah, New Jersey 07430

Printed and bound in the
United States of America

CONTENTS

Introduction	1
What is contemplation?	5
If contemplation is based on an interpersonal relationship with Jesus, and if it involves knowing him through love, what does this really mean for those of us wishing to be contemplative?	7
What does it mean to say, "Jesus loves me and Jesus loves you"?	9
How does Jesus love me?	10
Since everyone is called to grow in holiness, are we all called to contemplation?	13
What is contemplation supposed to "feel" like?	14
What are some ways to contemplate?	17
What can I learn from Mary as a model and teacher of contemplation?	24
How do I handle distractions in contemplation?	30

What is responsible for darkness and for desolation in contemplation, and what should I do when I experience them?	32
A few final words on contemplation.	34
Prayer for the gift of contemplation.	35
Suggestions for further reading.	36

INTRODUCTION

Probably one of the worst days you can pick to schedule a presentation in the United States is on the first Tuesday in September, the day after Labor Day. In most areas it is the first day of school; and so, most people are caught in the confusion that comes with the end of summer vacations and the beginning of a new academic or work year.

So, when a brief talk was scheduled at a small suburban Catholic college near Philadelphia on the day after Labor Day (1984), only two hundred and sixty chairs were set up. It was thought, "Surely that will be enough chairs . . . maybe too many." Yet, by the time the talk had started, all the available seats were occupied, the one hundred more that were hastily hauled up from the basement were quickly filled, and still forty more people wanting to attend ended up standing in the rear of the auditorium.

The room was filled with college administrators and faculty, school teachers and nurses, laborers and leaders of religious congregations. The crowd was genial but excited. The issue being discussed was of pressing concern to them. The topic? *Contemplating Jesus.*

Spiritual hunger knows no bounds. And the desire to learn how to be open to the grace of Jesus is of paramount concern to both the unschooled "street contemplative" and the prayerful theologian alike.

Still, though the topic was of real interest, given the terrible timing of the talk (and it had been raining earlier as well), the question still remained, "Why did so many people come?" After all, people not already schooled in prayer could probably pick up any one of the many books available on prayer, whereas certainly the spiritual directors and religious leaders in the audience would be thoroughly familiar with the information. So, why did they all come?

After talking with a number of the participants, the answer seemed clear: all present had a burning desire to view or renew their *basic* understanding of *contemplation*. For instance, for the people with a recent interest in being Jesus' friend or those wanting a little more guidance in getting better acquainted with him through prayer, there was an apparent need to hear a few simple reflections on how to know Jesus. To some in this group, the books available were too confusing or complex. Since they were not necessarily steeped in theology, but earnest in prayer, they just wanted a few words of direction to get them going, or, as some found out, to reaffirm that they were going in the right direction after all!

The second group—the spiritual directors, clergy, religious and those who were already well informed about prayer—also came for a primary, but slightly different, reason. They had a desire to get a brief, clear overview of the elementary aspects of contemplation so that it might serve as an organizing "window" to their approach in assisting others in prayer. Consequently, although they had been through many of the classics and contemporary works on prayer, they too wanted a brief return to the "basics." Like the novices in prayer present, they seemed drawn by the opportunity to appreciate the simplicity of contemplation.

Given these two reasons for interest in introductory material on contemplation, the basic considerations offered to the people present that evening are now put in written form for use by others with a similar interest or need: namely, to know Jesus, or to help others to know him better.

However, before presenting the following group of reflections and ideas on contemplation, several premises or biases underlying the comments to be made are offered in order to set the material in certain context. They are as follows:

(1) contemplation is a gift from God; we cannot earn it on our own;

(2) contemplation is really a *mystery* so although some comments can be made on it, little is actually known about it; and

(3) contemplation involves *relationship* . . . relationship with the Lord; and as in any relationship it takes time if it is to develop. Therefore, time must be set aside each day (30 minutes, 45 minutes, an hour . . .), preferably the same time, to be with the Lord to get to know him.

With these orienting points in mind then, the following brief practical synthesis of information on contemplation is offered with the hope that what is said can serve as a "preface" or "little companion" to the other available works on types of prayer.

What Is Contemplation?

To appreciate what contemplation is, there is a value in knowing what it is *not*. Contemplation is not prayer in terms of reasoning or of reflecting on the Gospel and applying it to my own life. Similarly, it is not thinking about the Lord, or even talking to the Lord in my own words.

Essentially, contemplation is non-conceptual prayer. In contemplation I spend time with Jesus. Quietly I am with the one I love, the one who loves me. Rather than trying to do something, I do little. It is his time. I let him lead; let him do with it what he wants.

Contemplation does not mean that I am thinking thoughts or that I am talking a lot. People sometimes pray as if they were "backseat drivers" and the Lord were behind the wheel; they give the Lord instructions and try to be forceful with words and actions even though they actually cannot control the contemplative process. In reality they would be better off in contemplation if they kept more silent and let the Lord lead.

Prayer is conversing with God. But, in contemplation, the conversation does not need a lot of words. It is a conversation that is somewhat "vague and murky." It is like being with someone whom I love and saying very little. When I am with someone I love, I do not have to talk all the time. And if you ask me what I am doing, I am going to have a good deal of trouble trying to explain it to you or giving you an account of my activity. All I know is that I am with someone I love, and that person is with me, and he or she loves me, and I love him or her, and the situation is that simple. The same can be said about being with Jesus in contemplation.

Contemplative prayer is also covenantal. It is a covenant, a relationship. God is in covenant with his people in the Old Testament; Jesus Christ is in covenant with the Church (Ephesians 5). Just as the Church is in covenant with Jesus Christ, so too I, as a Christian, am in covenant with him.

In contemplation I come more into awareness of my covenantal relationship with Jesus. That relationship becomes more conscious and so more human. In contemplation, I take the Lord seriously, and I put other things aside; I acknowledge his love for me by trying to love him back as best I can.

In contemplation the emphasis then is on *relationship*, relationship with the Lord. So, in contemplation I do not merely sit alone at home, in church, or in the corner of a room. Instead, I sit alone *with Jesus*. In contemplation I enter more deeply into a relationship with him. Rather than knowing *about* Jesus (which is properly gained through study, reflection and meditation), I seek to *know him* personally; and this knowing him is something that he alone can give.

Contemplation then is a gift of knowing Jesus as a person and of being there with him quietly in love. It is not just knowledge of Jesus that I seek; it is knowledge of Jesus *through love.* That is actually how I get to know the Lord in this life; I know him through love and that love basically is called the Holy Spirit. Essentially, the Holy Spirit is the mutual love between Jesus and the Father. The Father loves Jesus; Jesus loves the Father; and that mutual love between them is a Person, and that Person is the Holy Spirit who is sent into my heart relating me to the Father and to the Son. The result is: I am in relationship with God through the Holy Spirit who is love.

If contemplation is based on an interpersonal relationship with Jesus, and if it involves knowing him through love, what does this really mean for those of us wishing to be contemplative?

First of all, contemplation involves loving Jesus, and so it means a *commitment* to him. Now, compared to Jesus' love for me, my love is quite imperfect.

Everyone knows this; nevertheless, if I wish to have a life of contemplative prayer, to contemplate the Lord, I have to have a certain amount of commitment. I have to love him concretely; love is shown in deeds more than it is in words. In deeds—that is to say, I have to have time for the Lord everyday, a half hour, forty five minutes, or an hour, just being with the Lord in personal prayer.

If I really love the Lord, if I am committed to him and want to grow in my union with Jesus, then my commitment to him must be great enough that I give him a substantial amount of quiet time every day. Love is an expression of fidelity. It is good to tell the Lord that I love him; perhaps I do not do it enough. But real love is shown in faithfulness. And the kind of faithfulness the Lord calls me to is shown by spending some time with him everyday without fail. It is important.

I know Jesus through his love. He loves me. Jesus loves each one of us personally. Jesus knows my name. He knows everything about me: all my sins, all my defects, all my good qualities, all my hopes. He knows my past, my present and my future, and he accepts me without any conditions. He does not say, "I will love you more if you are better." He does not say, "Shape up and I will love you more." All he says is, "I love you just as you are; I would love you less if you were different." Out of all the possible "me's" and "you's", Jesus from the beginning of time saw me and you as we are right now. He picked us out of all the possible versions of us he could have created.

Jesus loves me. He does not love me because I am great; he really loves me because I am not. He did not come to save the just. He does not love me in spite of my sinfulness; he loves me partly *because* of my weakness, sinfulness, frailty; it is a characteristic in me to which he can respond with his compassion. My weakness and sinfulness provide the "opening" to his salvific love.

He loves us in the same way some parents love their retarded children more than their other children. A retarded child in a Christian family has such a strong character because he or she is loved so much. We are like the Lord's retarded children. Just as the way in which some parents love their retarded children, he loves us with a special compassion, care, and nurturing love. And he would love us less if we were different. Furthermore, when we appreciate this love as a retarded child in a loving family does, the result is beautiful.

What does it mean to say, "Jesus loves me and Jesus loves you"?

Asking this question is important because it is through love that I know Jesus in contemplation. Contemplation is, as has been noted previously *knowledge through love.* It is mainly through Jesus' love of me that I know him. I know him as the person who loves me most, who takes me most seriously. And, in response to this knowledge, I know that I am called to take him seriously, to love him back in a way that shows a concrete appreciation and recognition of the *fact* that he loves me.

How does Jesus love me?

One of the best ways to find out how Jesus loves me is to look at what he says about love. He teaches about love in the Sermon on the Mount. I can see what he says about how I am supposed to love others, and I can apply that to his love for me.

For example, in Luke's version of the Sermon on the Mount, Chapter Six, Jesus says, "Do not judge and you will not be judged." So, I know that Jesus will not judge me. "Do not condemn and you will not be condemned." So, I know that Jesus does not condemn me. Perhaps what I have done is so awful that I put it out of my consciousness so that I do not even get emotional about it anymore; but way down deep I think, "How could he ever forgive that?" Well, he does. He does not judge me and he does not condemn me. He says, "Forgive and you will be forgiven." So, I know that Jesus forgives me. No matter how many times I sin, he forgives me.

He also says, "Give and it will be given to you, full measure, pressed down and overflowing," so I know that Jesus gives to me. What does he give? Himself. He laid down his life for me as though I were the only other person who walked this earth. If I had been the only other person in the world, he would still have come and died for my salvation. He loves me with that kind of love, a self-giving love.

St. Paul talks about what love is in 1 Corinthians 13:4–7. It is helpful to look at this passage because it also describes what Jesus' love is for me and you.

> Love is patient; love is kind. Love is not jealous, it does not put on airs, it is not snobbish. Love is never rude, it is not self-seeking, it is not prone to anger; neither does it brood over injuries. Love does not rejoice in what is wrong but rejoices with the truth. There is no limit to love's forbearance, to its trust, its hope, its power to endure. (*New American Bible*)

That is how Jesus loves me . . . and loves *you!*

I know from Church teaching that Jesus is God, and I know from St. John's Gospel that God is love. Therefore, it is theologically correct to say that Jesus is love. And if Jesus is love, I can substitute Jesus' name for the word "love." The implications and import of this can be felt if I read the above passage doing this substitution, for then I will get a personality profile of Jesus with respect to his love for me. The answer to the question "What is the quality of Jesus' love for me?" will become particularly clear.

> *Jesus* is patient; Jesus is kind. Jesus is not jealous, he does not put on airs, he is not snobbish. Jesus is never rude, he is not self-seeking, he is not prone to anger. Jesus does not brood over injuries. Jesus does not rejoice in what is wrong; he rejoices with the truth. There is no limit to Jesus' forbearance, to his trust, to his hope, to his power to endure.

> "Lord Jesus, I thank you for being patient and kind with me, for bearing with me, for believing in me, for hoping in me, for being faithful to me no matter how unfaithful I have been. I thank you, Lord, because you do not insist on your own way. I thank you, Lord, because you are never irritable or put out with me. I ask you, Lord, to help me to be closer to you, especially to give me the grace of prayer, especially of the grace of contemplation so that I can know you better through love and, therefore, love you more and follow you more closely. Amen."

What is important in contemplation is the *heart*, not so much the head. It is the capacity to love. It is as I grow in union with the Lord—mainly through contemplative prayer—that I grow in the capacity to love and to receive love, that I grow in holiness. God is perfectly holy and he has an infinite capacity to love and receive love. He wants me to be holy—"Be perfect as your heavenly Father is perfect." How do I become holy? I become holy by growing in the capacity to love others and to receive love from others . . . especially the Lord. I grow by interacting with other people and trying to do the best I can in my family, with those with whom I work, play, live. However, the main source of growth still is contemplative prayer . . . quiet, loving union with Jesus—that is where I really grow in my capacity to give and to receive love.

Since everyone is called to grow in holiness, are we all called to contemplation?

Yes, all mature Christians are called to contemplation. There was a time when theologians discussed and disputed this issue. Now there seems to be unanimity on the question—*all* Christians are called to contemplative prayer. It is a gift and we are all called to receive it. Many of us think we are not the type. Yet, many of us who do not seem to resemble the quiet, reflective sort of person you think of when you hear the word "contemplation" (even the hyperactive and high-spirited who cannot seem to sit still for ten consecutive minutes) are able to receive the grace of contemplation. I certainly do not need to be a phlegmatic person to be a contemplative.

The Lord will quiet anyone who asks for the gift so that he or she can contemplate. The Lord gives the gift of contemplation to whomever he will. He wants to give it to everybody, and he offers it to everyone. I can ask him for the gift now. Say, "Lord, I am not very contemplative. I do not know how to pray. Teach me to pray; give me the gift of contemplation." And then start putting in a certain amount of time every day quietly being with Jesus in love, and see what happens. The simple truth is: if I ask him for the gift, he will give it to me, in his own way and in his own time.

What is contemplation supposed to "feel" like?

St. Ignatius Loyola helps answer this when he gives a criterion for prayer. The criterion is *consolation*. By that he means: facility in relating to the Lord. By "consolation" Ignatius also means feeling "right" in relationship with the Lord. Anything in the spectrum from feeling right, feeling peaceful, facility in relating to the Lord, to gladness, happiness, laughing out loud, and crying for joy can be included under the heading "consolation."

As a minimum, consolation means a certain *rightness*—in other words, I know the Lord is there. I may be in the dark. I may not feel the Lord's presence. I may not have any interior notion that he is there, *but* I know he is there. My prayer may be quite dry, quite dark. When I pray I feel down. When I try to say something, it sounds terrible. When I read the Bible, it does not seem to say much. It all seems to be a waste of time. It seems as though I am sitting in a chapel and nothing is happening, sitting in my room and nothing is going on, but I *know* the Lord is there. There is a basic peace. There is a basic facility in being with the Lord. I am quiet in the presence of the Lord because I know he is there; I know that he loves me and that is enough for me. He is working even if I do not feel it; and he is taking delight in me. And the work he does and the delight he takes in me effect results in me, even if I am not conscious of those results.

Or I might be happy, joyful, glad; I might have some awareness of the Lord's presence. But that is not essential. What is essential is the kind of basic peace the Lord gives. I can be in contemplation when the "lights are on" and I experience the Lord and I feel great; or I can have a dark contemplation. The same person will have different kinds of contemplation in different periods of his or her life.

Different things for different people, and different things for the same person at different times. At any rate, the essential thing in contemplative prayer is that the Lord is there and that I am there. I do not have to say much; he is doing the work. The Lord leads. Prayer is something like dancing. The Lord leads, and I follow. My part in contemplation is the passive part. I do not determine the kind or quality of the contemplative experience.

Or, again in line with the dance analogy, I do not determine whether the music is intense, slow, cheerful, or sad: I leave it to the Lord. He takes the active part. I follow him. If he is doing a "waltz," I do not want to be doing a "rhumba." I want to go the way he goes. And so I have to relax, open myself to spontaneity, and not try to program the Lord.

I can somewhat prepare my contemplation with the Lord the night before, but if I have it all lined up and expect him to follow all these "steps," he might not do it. He might, but I cannot count on it. The Lord leads and I have to let him love me the way he wants to love me at the time. So, the answer to the question "What should I do during contemplation?" is: whatever gives me the greatest facility in relating to the Lord, whatever (reading the Gospel, saying the rosary . . .) puts me most in touch with the Lord *at the time*. That is what I should do, because then I am going the way he is leading. How does he lead me? By giving me facility to be in relationship with him, and by giving me a certain feeling of rightness and interior peace in my relationship with him.

What are some ways to contemplate?

Before looking at several approaches to contemplation it is imperative that I clearly understand that it is not technique that counts in contemplation; it is *Jesus*. Technique is secondary. I do not really need a technique. If I want Jesus, I just go and be quiet in a certain place for a period of time and fill my heart with a deep desire to be closely united with him. If all I want is Jesus, some quiet time is all I actually need. I need only strip myself of everything, of all the junk, and be there as free as I can, and want the Lord. He will do the rest. He will lead. He will show me what to do. So, in looking at a number of helpful ways to approach contemplation, we must recognize that method is secondary. What is primary is, always: being with Jesus, looking at him with love.

A way of contemplation familiar to some people is what is referred to as "centering prayer." This prayer is far from new. Discussed clearly in the fourteenth century classic *The Cloud of Unknowing*, it no doubt dates back earlier than that time. It has affinities with Eastern Christianity and Hesychasm. It primarily consists of taking one word, "Jesus" for example, and repeating it silently in my heart very slowly, and using it as a way of centering on him. The center of my prayer in this instance is not the name of Jesus, but Jesus himself. I use his holy name as a way of centering myself on him. It is quite simple. Whole books have been written on this, but in fact it is quite straightforward. All I do is say the name of "Jesus" very slowly in my heart. It is not even so much that I say it, as it is that I let it, so to speak, say itself silently in my heart.

Another way to contemplate is to use the Gospel. For example, I can use a section of the Gospel of the day, or maybe work through an individual Gospel, one paragraph at a time, by reading just a few lines (five, six, ten) and use that, not as Bible study—although Bible study is good too—but as a way of relating to Jesus. The point is not that I remember what happened by reading the Bible, but that Jesus remembers. I ask to be taken into Jesus' risen heart to help me to understand what this text means for our relationship. So the point is not the literal meaning of the text; the point is to get to know Jesus and to use the text as a way of going to Jesus. I want to let him take me into his heart, into his memory, to show me what he wants to show me, to possibly help me to see the people and to hear what they were saying and to be part of what was actually going on. Or Jesus might want to help me just to know what the text means in terms of the relationship between us. Or he might lead me to be comfortable in relationships with him just resting quietly with the text, not to have any ideas or words, but just resting in the Lord.

I can also use the Bible as a centering prayer. I can read the text slowly, maybe spending a little time letting it sink in. And then I can close the Bible and just sink into the text without thinking about it, without reflecting on it, without trying to apply it to my life. I can go quietly to the Lord in terms of the text, resting there with that text. And at the same time, I can use the name of Jesus as a centering prayer, repeating the word "Jesus" silently and slowly in my heart.

Another way to contemplate is to say the rosary. The rosary is basically a contemplative prayer. No matter where I go in the world, in any large city, I can usually find one or two elderly people in the back of a downtown church praying the rosary. Some of these people have very high contemplative prayer. Although they have the rosaries in their hands and know how to say the prayers, they are *not thinking* about the individual "Our Fathers" and "Hail Marys" that they are saying. They are looking at Jesus in the mysteries of his life and death and resurrection. They are in contemplation. They reached this point probably over a long period of time. With the Lord's grace, with the help of his Holy Spirit, they are just looking at the Lord with love. The rosary, used in this way, is a good way to contemplate the Lord.

Another way to contemplation, which does not apply to everybody (and may even raise resistance in some people), is praying in tongues. Praying in tongues is part of the pentecostal or charismatic movement. However, what is not generally known is that this type of prayer is, by no means, restricted to this movement. Many people, even many who would not classify themselves as "charismatic" or "pentecostal," pray in tongues as a way of contemplating Jesus. The main use of praying or singing in tongues is in one's personal prayer. St. Paul says just that in 1 Corinthians 13: "When I pray in tongues I speak to God." The main use of tongues, though certainly used beneficially in group worship, is really in personal prayer. (As a matter of fact, you may be surprised to find out that many people who pray in tongues have never been to a pentecostal or charismatic meeting and they have no inclination to do so.)

When I pray in tongues, do I understand what I am saying or singing? No. When I pray in tongues, I do not speak a real language, except perhaps in exceptional cases. The syllables do not have any conceptual content; they have no meaning. There is nothing to understand. When I pray in tongues, I look simply at the Lord, in love, and babble to him, like a baby who does not yet know how to talk. Prayer in tongues is not a real language like, say, English or Italian; it is a language the way dancing and painting are languages.

Praying in tongues is "vocalized contemplation." Just as there is a silent contemplation, a silent looking at Jesus with love, so too there are vocalized forms of contemplation. The rosary is one vocalized form of contemplation; speaking in tongues is another. Speaking in tongues is noisy contemplation.

It is a way to keep myself on the track, like centering prayer, or like saying the rosary. It is a way of avoiding distractions. It is a way of looking at Jesus with love without thoughts or ideas. I just babble to the Lord and look at him with love; that is what I do when I pray in tongues.

If I want the gift of tongues and I do not have it, how do I get it? Generally there are three types of people: first, those who pray in tongues and use it in prayer; second, those who are turned off by the whole idea; third, those who do not pray in tongues but think they might like to. If I am in the third category I have two options. The first is that I can go to somewhere private, where I am alone (maybe the privacy of my room), kneel down, and ask the Lord for the gift of tongues. Having done this I then make an act of faith, look at Jesus with love, open my mouth and start babbling or singing like a baby that does not know how to talk yet. I let it flow, singing or speaking tongues, looking at the Lord with love and singing or speaking to him—babbling to him. My pride may, in the beginning, cause me to feel foolish; but that will pass.

Another approach is to go to someone who has the gift of tongues and to ask him or her to pray with me for the gift. Praying in tongues is, for many, a good way to pray. Many people, for instance, note that they have experienced a real breakthrough in their relationship with the Lord after having received this gift.

Another way to contemplate Jesus is to take your decisions to him. Review the decisions you have to make. Take the "pros" and "cons" to the Lord, and then just sit there looking at Jesus weighing both sides and seeing which side of the equation, which option or which decision you are most comfortable with; it is a way of both contemplating Jesus and trying to see how he feels on different decisions you might make.

Finally I can contemplate Jesus as healer, as the one who heals me. I can take my hurts to him. I can take my negative feelings to him—including the ones about him or about my relationship with him. I can take my inner turmoil, anger, resentment, fear or negative feelings of any kind. I can take these to the Lord, and I do not have to say anything. I can just let the Lord hold me and put his arms around me, comfort me, console me and heal me. Jesus the healer is always available to heal me. I need only to open myself to him quietly by just being there with him in contemplative prayer, trying to receive his love, responding to it in any bumbling way that I can, just letting the Lord look at me with love, with all of the benevolence that he has for me.

Hurts can come up as distractions in my prayer. Perhaps someone has hurt me, recently, or in the past, and the hurt comes to the surface in my prayer as a distraction. I can forgive that person in my heart. And I can then turn to the Lord and ask him to heal the hurt.

In some ways it is hard to talk about inner healing because the Lord sometimes heals me of hurts I do not even know I have. Being with Jesus and receiving his love and opening my heart to his love and letting him look at me with love, and letting him—so to speak—put his arms around me, that is healing, and that is what I do when I look at Jesus with love, when I contemplate Jesus.

Even if I do not ask for healing in any explicit way, it is a healing experience. He heals me through his love. That is what he does in the Gospels. He casts out evil spirits; he heals people; he raises people from the dead. Why? Because he loves them. It is the love in him, the love that is the Holy Spirit, the Spirit of Jesus, that is so powerful.

The love that Jesus has for me is a powerful love. It is more than I need. It is more than I need to heal me, to make me holy, to lead me in the way of prayer, to help me to be a good Christian and disciple of Jesus. All I have to do is go to him, look at him with love, with the "eyes" of the heart, and let him do it . . . and he will.

What can I learn from Mary as a model and teacher of contemplation?

As can be seen in the Gospels, Mary is a model of both contemplation and discipleship. The classic Gospel of Mary is the first part of Luke's Gospel. All through that Gospel, whenever Luke refers to Mary he talks about her as the ideal disciple. Mary is not only the mother of Jesus, she is also his disciple; and, as we know, at the heart of discipleship is contemplation. This contemplation on Mary's part took many forms, but in all instances it reflects the basic element needed in the contemplative way of knowing Jesus—namely, looking at Jesus with love.

When we look at the baroque paintings of the nativity of the late seventeenth century and early eighteenth century, we often see portrayals of the holy family. And in many of them Mary is looking at Jesus with love; that is contemplation. At Cana, in John's Gospel, Mary again looks at Jesus, but with a different kind of contemplation. It is a lament, a petition. She says to the Lord, "They have no wine." What is she doing? Softly complaining. She outlines very briefly the situation: they drank all the wine. Then what does she do? (We can imagine it by reading between the lines.) She looks at Jesus—not to see what he is going to do, because she knows what he is going to do; she just looks at him with great love and trust because she knows that he is going to handle the situation. She may not know how, but she knows he is going to take care of it. Love is trusting, dependent. She is sure he loves her and she knows she loves him. Her looking at Jesus is contemplation as petition.

At the foot of the cross, Mary is contemplative; what is she doing? Looking at Jesus with love, sharing his passion. She suffers with Jesus; she is in a dark contemplation, a contemplation without happy feelings. It is a great sadness, a terrible overpowering sadness, and it is utter darkness. It is the hour of the power of evil; yet she is there with him in that darkness.

Mary, then, is both the model and the teacher of contemplation. We learn from her by looking at her and then by doing what she does.

What does she do? She does not say much. She looks at the Lord with love. The Magnificat (Mary's song of praise—in the first part of Luke's Gospel), for example, is practically a program for contemplative prayer. It is a lesson in contemplation in that it provides the qualities of contemplative prayer. By doing a "spiritual exegesis" of this prayer I can gain practical insights into contemplation. That is to say, by not doing a literal interpretation or contextual examination of this Gospel passage, but rather by seeking an application of what Mary says in the Magnificat to me, here and now in my situation (and my situation now is that I am interested in contemplation), I can gain knowledge about knowing Jesus through love.

What the Magnificat says to me about Mary as a model of contemplation can be learned by looking at the passage:

> About the same time Mary set out in haste to a Judean town in the hill country. She entered Zechariah's house and greeted Elizabeth. When Mary greeted Elizabeth, the child in her womb leapt. Elizabeth was filled with the Holy Spirit and uttered in a loud voice, "Blessed indeed are you among women, and blessed is the Fruit of your womb, but why should this happen to me that the mother of my Lord God come to me? For as the sound of your greeting reached my ears the child in my womb leapt with delight. Blessed indeed is the woman who has believed." (Luke 1:39–45)

Now, I need only look closer at this passage with a "spiritual eye" toward how Mary is the model and teacher of contemplation and much can be learned.

Mary is described by Luke as "the woman who has believed," a model of discipleship. She is the believer *par excellence*. She believes that what the Lord has promised her will see fulfillment.

Then Mary says, "My soul declares the greatness of the Lord." Or, in the RSV translation, "My soul magnifies the Lord." That is the first thing about contemplation; it magnifies the Lord. Contemplation, with few words, as non-conceptual prayer, is paying attention to the Lord: paying attention to him; magnifying him with an attention that has a special quality. What quality? Reverence, because God is God. So, when I look at him with love I am also looking with reverence. It is an attention that magnifies, one that declares the Lord's greatness, that professes his greatness, that applauds it, that takes him seriously . . . and this takes few or no words. After all, there is not a whole lot of room for words. What are you going to say? No matter how eloquent the praise, after a point it breaks down. It becomes inadequate. If you really take Jesus seriously for who he is, risen and present God, there is little—almost nothing!—to say. Just looking at him, taking him seriously, being in his presence, that is the first quality of contemplation.

And the second is here in one of Mary's other statements, "My spirit finds delight in God my Savior." What does that mean for us? It means that contemplation rejoices in God my Savior, contemplation takes delight in God my Savior. Does that mean that contemplation always has to be happy? No, contemplation can sometimes be and sometimes is like Mary at the foot of the cross. It just means that there is at least some minimal joy, some kind of peace, present in contemplation unless there is a problem. As indicated before, normally I should have at least what St. Ignatius calls "consolation," facility in relating to the Lord.

Mary says, as she goes on in the Magnificat, "My spirit finds delight in God my Savior, because he has had regard for the lowliness of his handmaiden." He has looked upon the lowliness of Mary; so lowliness is an important quality of contemplation. Why were not the scribes and the Pharisees contemplatives? They looked at Jesus and they did not like what they saw. They certainly did not look at Jesus with love. Most of them looked at Jesus with fear and intimidation because they were not lowly. *They could not be small enough to be contemplatives.*

What I want in contemplation is the lowliness of Mary, the kind of humility that is a receptivity for contemplation as a passive state. It is a receptive state. It is a state where I receive the Lord and the power of his love. The Lord will come to me; because he did not come to save the upright and the just, he came to save the lowly and the sinners. He said, "It is not the well that have need for a doctor, it is the sick" (Luke 9:12). And so, I need to recognize my own sinfulness, my own spiritual sickness and my own inadequacy in order to pray and to be open to the Spirit that Jesus wants to send me.

It is not necessary to pray well. We all just sort of bumble along, doing our best, praying any way we can. And the Lord looks at us in our lowliness and he has mercy on us—not in spite of our sinfulness, not in spite of our weakness, but partly because of those very things. Did he love Mary Magdalene less because she was a prostitute? No. No one who reads about Mary Magdalene in the Bible would say "yes" to that.

Essentially, then, when I approach Jesus he looks upon my lowliness, and this lowliness accepted by me turns into a receptivity to his compassion, to his love. This helps me enter into a contemplative relationship with him.

Mary continues, "The Almighty has done great things for me." He who is mighty has done great things for me, and that is the secret of contemplation. The Lord does it. When I contemplate, most of the prayer is from him, not from me. I am the receiver; he is the giver. And what he is giving me may be extremely difficult to describe or to define. This is because he is giving me himself.

When a person gives himself or herself to me in love, I cannot put him or her in categories; I cannot tap the mystery of the depth of the person. So too I cannot fathom the greatest person, the greatest mystery . . . Jesus. God understands me, yet he does not expect me to perfectly understand him, just to accept him, to take seriously the mystery of his personhood and the mystery of his love. In response to this attitude and fidelity on my part, he does it, he leads, he guides my prayer.

> "Mary, I ask you to intercede for me now for the graces of contemplative prayer. I ask you to intercede for me so that the Almighty can do great things for me in my prayer, so that he can look on my lowliness and help me to accept my own sinfulness. I know Jesus loves me not in spite of my sinfulness but partly because of it. Help me, and pray that I receive the graces that will lead me to a peace and a joy and a rightness in the Lord Jesus so my soul can magnify him the same way yours does. Amen."

How do I handle distractions in contemplation?

Distractions can and do bother most people at some time in contemplation. They can be related to people (somebody I resent or with whom I am angry, someone I have a lot of affection for, someone who may be ill or in trouble . . .) and things (i.e., finances, projects, my work). Such distractions occur when a person or thing is not integrated into my relationship with the Lord. If it were integrated into my relationship with Jesus, then it would not be a distraction; it would lead me into union with him, not away from him. Therefore, when I have a continual distraction, I need to take steps to bring it into my life with the Lord, not by trying to suppress it, but by lifting it up to the Lord in prayer. The result is that instead of it remaining solely part of *my* life, it becomes part of *our* (the Lord's and my) life. The issue then ceases to remain on the fringe of our relationship. Instead, my bringing it to the Lord and giving it to him while I look at him in love serves to further cement our relationship. It makes that relationship more real, more vital.

Also, in such instances, the Lord will take care of the things I bring to him. Although the problems, attachments, or issues may not disappear, they can take on a new perspective. As a matter of fact, the movement of distractions from the surface of my prayer to their ultimate integration into my life with the Lord is one of the very processes by which forward movement in relationship with Jesus takes place.

If there is something askew in my life—some inappropriate attachment which preoccupies me—it will inevitably turn up in prayer. When it does, I should put it in Jesus' hands; that is one of the ways he leads me to get my whole life centered on him. He wants to be Lord of my *whole* life—all my relationships, all my problems (money, people, health), all my concerns; he wants me to center all of it on him. Whatever is not centered on him will come up as a distraction in prayer.

With this type of understanding of what distractions in contemplation are, I can feel a freedom and sense of acceptance in bringing them into my relationship with the Lord. I can see the need to present them to him while I look at him in love and with the faith that he will take care of them. Through this movement more and more we—Jesus and I—become one.

What is responsible for darkness and for desolation in contemplation, and what should I do when I experience them?

My contemplation might be, so to speak, in darkness, "lights out," a desert experience of dryness. This darkness or dryness can be a purifying grace from the Lord. I can accept that darkness or dryness, and rest peacefully in the Lord.

Contemplation can also be accompanied by real misery. I think everyone of us who prays has experienced this. In such an instance, I have a feeling of desolation in contemplation. In a word, I feel miserable.

The question is: Is all of this really from the Lord? Well, the night may be from the Lord, the darkness can be from the Lord, but not the misery, not the desolation.

So, what do I have to do? Well, just work through it. Ride it out. If the cause of the misery can be identified, deal with it. And stay faithful to prayer. Then, maybe the lights will not go on immediately, but the darkness will not make me feel so miserable.

So, there is a distinction between darkness and desolation. Contemplation can very often be dark but it does not have to be desolate for a long period of time. With patience, perseverance and love, I can come out of desolation (hopefully the sooner the better) and into a peace and a feeling of rightness with the Lord, letting him continue to purify me but with not so much misery.

A FEW FINAL WORDS ON CONTEMPLATION

Taking the Lord seriously with reverent attention and, secondly, rightness or a feeling of peace that can also be a feeling of happiness—these are the two essential qualities of contemplation. They represent the basic elements of the *gift* of contemplation, the gift that the Lord gives me when I take out time each day to be with him in the Spirit of love. All of the previous comments made on contemplating Jesus then, although trying to be of some guidance in moving us toward the Lord, really come down to this:

> If I ask for the gift of contemplation, and I start spending a certain amount of time each day quietly looking at Jesus with love, the gift of contemplation, and growth in that gift, will be given to me. If and when I am distracted, discouraged, dry, and almost desolate in prayer, I can throw myself on the Lord's mercy. Jesus is faithful.

Prayer for the Gift of Contemplation

"Jesus, I do ask you for the graces of prayer, especially for the grace of contemplative union with you. Teach me, Jesus, to know you better, so that I can love you more and follow you more closely. Teach me to take you seriously, as the person in my life who takes me most seriously, understands me perfectly, and loves me without any conditions. Lord Jesus, I give you my heart; I ask you to change it and to teach me to pray. Amen."

SUGGESTIONS FOR FURTHER READING

The best book to read for anything involving the Lord, including the gift of contemplation, is of course the Bible. You might find particularly helpful: The Gospel of Luke, Chapter 10, verse 38, to Chapter 11, verse 13; The Gospel of Matthew, Chapter 6, verses 5 to 15; Paul's Letter to the Romans, Chapter 8; and Psalm 139, verses 1 to 18. The traditional classic works on contemplation are as valid as ever, especially: Teresa of Avila, *The Interior Castle;* and John of the Cross, *The Ascent of Mount Carmel,* and *The Dark Night.*

Here are some contemporary books you might find helpful:

Burrows, Ruth. *Guidelines for Mystical Prayer.* London: Sheed and Ward, 1976.

Faricy, Robert. *Seeking Jesus in Contemplation and Discernment.* Wilmington, DE: Michael Glazier, 1983.

Green, Thomas H. *When the Well Runs Dry.* Notre Dame: Ave Maria Press, 1981.

———. *Opening to Prayer.* Notre Dame: Ave Maria Press, 1977.

Wicks, Robert J. *Availability: The Problem and the Gift.* Mahwah, NJ: Paulist, 1986.